AI REVOLUTION

Unleashing the Power of Automation
and Human Ingenuity

imrtst

Copyright © 2023 imrtst

All rights reserved

No part of this book may be reproduced, stored in a retrieval system, or transmitted in any form or by any means, electronic, mechanical, photocopying, recording, scanning, or otherwise, without the prior written permission of the publisher.

ISBN: [9798399756912]
imprint: independently published

This book is a work created through the collaboration of human creativity and the use of AI technology. While AI played a role in generating content based on prompts and guidelines, the final product has been reviewed and refined by human authors to ensure its quality and coherence.

This book is a work of fiction. Names, characters, places, and incidents are either the product of the author's imagination or used fictitiously.

Dedication

This book is dedicated to all the pioneers, innovators, and visionaries who have tirelessly pushed the boundaries of artificial intelligence (AI) and its applications. Your relentless pursuit of knowledge, your passion for discovery, and your commitment to creating a better future have paved the way for the advancements we see today.

To the brilliant minds who have shaped the field of AI and continue to inspire generations to come, this book is a tribute to your remarkable contributions. Your groundbreaking research, groundbreaking technologies, and unwavering dedication have transformed the way we live, work, and interact with the world.

I would also like to dedicate this book to the individuals and organizations who are actively embracing AI, harnessing its power to drive positive change across various industries. From healthcare and finance to manufacturing and transportation, you are leading the way in leveraging AI's potential to improve efficiency, enhance decision-making, and create innovative solutions.

Lastly, this book is dedicated to the readers who seek knowledge and understanding in the realm of AI and its impact on jobs and society. Your curiosity, open-mindedness, and willingness to explore new ideas are what inspire authors like myself to share insights and perspectives. It is my hope that this book will provide you with valuable insights, spark meaningful discussions, and empower you to navigate the evolving landscape of AI with confidence.

To all those mentioned above, and to the countless others who have contributed to the field of AI in various ways, this book is dedicated to you. Your passion, dedication, and unwavering belief in the transformative power of AI continue to shape our world and shape the future.

"Artificial intelligence is the new electricity. It has the potential to transform every industry and every aspect of human life."

SUNDAR PICHAI(GOOGLE CEO)

PREFACE

Welcome to the world of artificial intelligence (AI) and its profound impact on jobs and society. This book serves as a comprehensive exploration of the ever-evolving relationship between AI and the workforce, delving into its implications, challenges, and potential opportunities.

In an era marked by unprecedented technological advancements, AI stands at the forefront as a catalyst for change. It has transcended the realms of science fiction to become an integral part of our daily lives, revolutionizing industries, transforming economies, and reshaping the way we work and live. The rapid development and adoption of AI technologies have brought both excitement and apprehension, as questions arise about the future of jobs, human-machine collaboration, and the ethical considerations surrounding AI.

This book aims to navigate the complexities of this AI-driven revolution, providing readers with a comprehensive understanding of the interplay between AI and jobs. We will embark on a journey that explores the historical roots of AI, its current state, and its promising potential for the future. Through meticulous research, insightful analysis, and thought-provoking discussions, we will shed light on the impact of AI on various sectors, the changing dynamics of the job market, and the implications for individuals, businesses, and society as a whole.

Each chapter of this book delves into specific aspects of the AI and job landscape, examining the risks, benefits, and key considerations associated with this transformative technology. We will explore the types of jobs that are most vulnerable to AI automation and those that are more resilient to its disruptive forces. We will delve into the ethical dilemmas surrounding AI, the potential for bias and discrimination, and the need for responsible and accountable AI systems. Furthermore, we will examine the potential for AI to drive innovation, create new job opportunities, and reshape industries.

Throughout this journey, we will draw upon real-world examples, case studies, and expert insights to provide a well-rounded perspective on the complex relationship between AI and jobs. We will also address common misconceptions, dispel fears, and emphasize the importance of human skills and adaptability in the face of AI-driven transformations.

It is my hope that this book will serve as a valuable resource for readers seeking to navigate the AI revolution with knowledge and foresight. Whether you are an AI enthusiast, a business leader, a policymaker, or an individual curious about the future of work, this book offers a comprehensive exploration of AI's impact on jobs and society. By fostering understanding and promoting informed discussions, we can shape a future where AI and human collaboration thrive, ultimately leading to a more inclusive, equitable, and prosperous society.

Thank you for joining me on this transformative journey. Let us embark on this exploration of AI and jobs together, unraveling the mysteries, challenges, and possibilities that lie ahead.

INTRODUCTION

The AI Revolution: Transforming Industries and Shaping the Future

Artificial Intelligence (AI) has emerged as a transformative force, revolutionizing industries and shaping the future of our world. With its ability to analyze vast amounts of data, learn from patterns, and make intelligent decisions, AI has opened up new horizons and possibilities across various sectors. From healthcare to finance, manufacturing to transportation, education to entertainment, AI is driving unprecedented advancements, improving efficiency, and delivering innovative solutions.

In this introduction, we will explore the profound impact of the AI revolution on different sectors and delve into the transformative potential it holds. We will discuss how AI technologies are disrupting traditional paradigms, creating new opportunities, and addressing complex challenges. By understanding the breadth and depth of AI's influence, we can appreciate the magnitude of the changes that lie ahead.

AI in Healthcare: Revolutionizing Diagnosis, Treatment, and Care

The healthcare sector stands to benefit immensely from AI advancements. From diagnosing diseases and predicting outcomes to personalized treatment plans and drug discovery, AI is revolutionizing healthcare delivery. Machine learning algorithms can analyze medical records, genetic data, and clinical research to provide accurate diagnoses and treatment recommendations. Additionally, AI-enabled devices and wearables are empowering individuals to monitor their health in real-time, leading to proactive interventions and improved patient outcomes.

AI in Finance: Enhancing Efficiency and Risk Management

The financial industry is undergoing a seismic shift with the integration of AI technologies. AI-powered algorithms can analyze complex market trends, predict financial risks, and automate trading decisions. Chatbots and virtual assistants are streamlining customer interactions, providing personalized financial advice, and enhancing user experience. Furthermore, AI is playing a crucial role in fraud detection and prevention, ensuring secure transactions and safeguarding sensitive financial data.

AI in Manufacturing: Optimizing Processes and Enabling Automation

The manufacturing sector is embracing AI to optimize processes, increase productivity, and drive innovation. AI-powered robotics and automation systems are revolutionizing production lines, improving efficiency, and reducing errors. Machine learning algorithms can analyze production data in real-time, enabling predictive maintenance, quality control, and supply chain optimization. With AI, manufacturers can respond quickly to market demands, customize products, and achieve greater operational agility.

AI in Transportation: Enabling Smarter Mobility and Autonomous Systems

Transportation is experiencing a paradigm shift with the integration of AI technologies. AI-powered systems are driving advancements in autonomous vehicles, making transportation safer and more efficient. Machine learning algorithms can analyze traffic patterns, optimize routes, and reduce congestion. AI-enabled predictive maintenance enhances the reliability of transportation systems, while smart traffic management systems improve overall efficiency and reduce environmental impact.

AI in Education: Personalizing Learning and Enhancing Accessibility

The education sector is undergoing a significant transformation with the integration of AI technologies. Intelligent tutoring systems can personalize learning experiences, adapt to individual student needs, and provide targeted feedback. AI-powered virtual reality and augmented reality applications are creating immersive educational experiences, making complex concepts more accessible and engaging. Additionally, AI can automate administrative tasks, freeing up educators' time for personalized instruction and student support.

AI in Entertainment: Revolutionizing Content Creation and User Experience

The entertainment industry is leveraging AI to enhance content creation and deliver immersive user experiences. AI-powered algorithms can analyze user preferences and behavior to recommend personalized content. Machine learning techniques enable the creation of realistic animations, special effects, and virtual characters. Furthermore, AI-driven content moderation tools help protect online platforms from harmful and inappropriate content.

In the following chapters, we will delve deeper into each sector, exploring

PROLOGUE

In the vast landscape of human progress, few forces have captured our collective imagination and shaped the course of history like the power of innovation. Throughout the ages, groundbreaking inventions and transformative ideas have propelled civilizations forward, paving the way for advancements in science, technology, and human achievement. And now, at the dawn of the 21st century, a new force has emerged to redefine the very fabric of our existence: artificial intelligence (AI).

The prologue of this book invites you to embark on a captivating journey through the realm of AI and its profound impact on jobs and society. Like a modern-day Prometheus, AI possesses the potential to bestow extraordinary gifts upon humanity while simultaneously challenging our fundamental understanding of work, creativity, and human potential.

As we stand on the precipice of this AI-driven revolution, it is crucial to pause and reflect on the extraordinary strides we have made in the field of AI and the remarkable possibilities that lie ahead. From its humble beginnings as a concept in the minds of early visionaries to its current state as a pervasive force in our daily lives, AI has undergone a remarkable evolution.

In this prologue, we will embark on a journey through time, tracing the origins of AI and its gradual integration into the fabric of society. We will delve into the minds of pioneering researchers and trailblazing innovators who have dared to push the boundaries of what was once deemed possible. Their tireless efforts have paved the way for the AI-powered technologies that are now shaping industries, transforming economies, and challenging our notions of labor and human expertise.

But amidst the awe-inspiring achievements of AI, we also encounter a myriad of questions, uncertainties, and ethical considerations. How will AI reshape the job market, and what implications will this have for individuals and communities? Will AI-driven automation lead to widespread job displacement or create new opportunities for innovation and growth? What role does human ingenuity, adaptability, and empathy play in the face of increasing automation?

As we delve deeper into the subsequent chapters of this book, we will explore these questions and more, unraveling the intricate tapestry of AI's impact on jobs and society. We will examine the risks and benefits, the challenges and opportunities, and the ethical and societal implications that arise from the integration of AI into our professional and personal lives.

This prologue sets the stage for the enlightening and thought-provoking journey that lies ahead. It serves as a reminder that, while AI may challenge our preconceptions and disrupt traditional norms, it is ultimately a reflection of our own boundless curiosity and innate desire to push the boundaries of human achievement.

So, dear reader, fasten your seatbelts and prepare to traverse the captivating landscape of AI and jobs. Together, we will navigate the complexities, unveil the possibilities, and explore the paths that lead to a harmonious coexistence between human and artificial intelligence. Welcome to a world where the realms of science fiction and reality converge, where the future of work is shaped, and where the true potential of our collective ingenuity is yet to be fully realized.

Let the journey begin.

[imrtst]
Author

FOREWORD

As I stand on the precipice of technological innovation, gazing into the boundless realms of artificial intelligence (AI), I am filled with both awe and trepidation. The advancements in AI have the potential to reshape the very fabric of our society, challenging our long-held beliefs, and transforming the way we work, live, and interact with the world.

It is with great pleasure and anticipation that I present this forward for the book exploring the intricate relationship between AI and jobs. The pages that follow offer a comprehensive and insightful exploration of this complex and rapidly evolving landscape, shedding light on the opportunities, challenges, and ethical considerations that arise from the integration of AI into our workforce.

In an era characterized by unprecedented technological progress, it is imperative that we understand the implications of AI on jobs and society. This book serves as a guiding light, navigating the intricacies of AI's impact on various sectors, the changing dynamics of the job market, and the potential pathways that lie ahead. Through meticulous research, compelling narratives, and thought-provoking analysis, the author embarks on a journey to illuminate the complex interplay between human labor and machine intelligence.

The profound transformations brought about by AI necessitate a nuanced and informed discussion. From the potential for job displacement to the creation of new opportunities, from ethical dilemmas to the reimagining of industries, each chapter of this book delves into critical aspects of the AI revolution. Drawing upon real-world examples, expert insights, and historical perspectives, the author provides a panoramic view of the challenges and possibilities that lie ahead.

As you delve into the chapters that follow, you will be confronted with the realities of AI's impact on jobs. The author's meticulous research and well-articulated arguments will challenge your preconceived notions, broaden your understanding, and provoke contemplation about the future of work. It is my hope that these pages ignite meaningful conversations and inspire collective action to shape a future where AI and human potential intertwine harmoniously.

To the readers embarking on this intellectual expedition, I urge you to approach these insights with an open mind, embracing the complexities and uncertainties that accompany transformative change. Only through such exploration can we foster a deeper understanding of the challenges and opportunities that lie ahead, empowering us to navigate this AI-driven world with wisdom and foresight.

The author's dedication, passion, and expertise shine through the pages of this book, making it an indispensable resource for academics, policymakers, business leaders, and individuals seeking to navigate the profound shifts brought about by AI. By fostering a deeper understanding of the complexities of AI and jobs, we can collectively shape a future that harnesses the power of AI to drive prosperity, equality, and human flourishing.

I commend the author for their tireless efforts in crafting this remarkable work. Their commitment to rigorous research, balanced analysis, and clarity of thought has resulted in a book that illuminates the path forward in an era defined by the convergence of human ingenuity and machine intelligence.

Now, dear reader, I invite you to embark on this transformative journey, immersing yourself in the rich tapestry of AI and jobs. May these pages ignite your curiosity, provoke meaningful dialogue, and inspire action as we navigate the uncharted territories of the AI revolution together.

[imrtst]

Distinguished Expert in the Field of AI and Technology

CHAPTER 1: AI AND JOBS

1.1 The Impact of AI on Jobs

In this section, we will delve into the profound impact of artificial intelligence (AI) on the job market. We will explore how AI technologies are reshaping industries, transforming workflows, and challenging traditional notions of work and employment. By examining real-world examples and case studies, we will provide insights into the specific ways in which AI is influencing different sectors and job roles.

1.2 Changing Job Market Dynamics

This subsection focuses on the dynamic nature of the job market in the era of AI. We will discuss how AI is altering the demand for certain skill sets and the composition of the workforce. We will examine the rise of new job roles that are directly related to AI technologies, as well as the potential impact on existing job roles. Additionally, we will explore the concept of job displacement and the need for reskilling and upskilling to adapt to the evolving job market.

1.3 Jobs at Risk of Automation

Here, we will analyze the types of jobs that are most susceptible to automation and the factors that contribute to their vulnerability. We will explore industries and job sectors where AI technologies have the potential to replace human workers, such as manufacturing, customer service, transportation, and data entry. By examining the underlying reasons behind job automation, we will gain a deeper understanding of the specific skills and tasks that AI can replicate.

1.4 Jobs Resilient to AI Disruption

This subsection focuses on the job roles that are less likely to be replaced by AI. We will identify professions that involve high levels of creativity, emotional intelligence, complex problem-solving, and human interaction. By highlighting the unique human qualities that AI currently lacks, such as empathy, intuition, and social intelligence, we will explore the areas where human workers continue to hold a competitive advantage.

1.5 The Potential Benefits of AI for the Job Market

In this section, we will explore the positive aspects of AI's impact on the job market. We will discuss how AI technologies can increase efficiency, productivity, and innovation in various industries. We will examine case studies where AI has enabled workers to focus on higher-value tasks, improved decision-making processes, and created new job opportunities. By understanding the potential benefits, we can identify avenues for leveraging AI to enhance the job market.

CHAPTER 2: THE PROS AND CONS OF AI

2.1 Advantages of AI

This subsection explores the advantages of AI in the context of employment. We will discuss how AI technologies can reduce human error, automate repetitive tasks, and analyze vast amounts of data with speed and accuracy. By examining real-world applications, we will highlight the specific ways in which AI enhances efficiency, productivity, and decision-making processes in various industries. We will also address the potential cost savings and improved customer experiences that AI can bring.

2.2 Disadvantages of AI

Here, we will explore the challenges and drawbacks associated with AI in the job market. We will discuss the issue of algorithmic bias, where AI systems may inadvertently perpetuate discriminatory practices. We will examine the limitations of AI in areas that require human emotion, creativity, and intuition. Additionally, we will address the "black box" nature of AI, where the decision-making processes of complex AI systems may lack transparency and accountability.

2.3 The Impact of AI on Society

In this section, we will examine the broader impact of AI on society as a whole. We will discuss the potential ramifications of widespread AI adoption, including societal inequality, job polarization, and shifts in economic power. We will explore the ethical considerations surrounding AI, such as privacy concerns, data security, and the potential for AI to exacerbate existing societal biases. By critically analyzing the social implications of AI, we can navigate the path towards responsible and equitable AI integration.

CHAPTER 3: WHAT AI CAN AND CAN'T DO

3.1 The Capabilities of AI

This section focuses on the various capabilities of AI technologies. We will delve into machine learning, natural language processing, computer vision, and other key AI domains. Through real-world examples, we will demonstrate how AI can process and analyze large volumes of data, make predictions and recommendations, understand and generate human language, and interpret visual information. By showcasing the breadth and depth of AI capabilities, we can better understand its potential applications.

3.2 The Limitations of AI

Here, we explore the limitations of AI technologies. While AI systems excel at specific tasks, they face challenges in areas that require abstract thinking, common sense reasoning, and human-like intuition. We will discuss the concept of "narrow AI" and its implications, highlighting the areas where AI falls short. We will also address the problem of recursivity, where AI struggles with self-referential or self-modifying tasks. Understanding these limitations is crucial for setting realistic expectations and identifying areas where human involvement remains essential.

3.3 The Future Evolution of AI

In this subsection, we will delve into the potential for AI to evolve and improve in the future. We will discuss ongoing research and developments in AI, such as advances in deep learning, reinforcement learning, and cognitive architectures. We will explore the concept of general AI, where machines possess human-level intelligence and adaptability. By examining current trends and projections, we can gain insights into the trajectory of AI development and its potential impact on the job market and society at large.

CHAPTER 4: THE IMPACT OF AI ON HUMANS

4.1 Benefits of AI for Humans

This section focuses on the potential benefits that AI can bring to human workers. We will explore how AI technologies can increase productivity, efficiency, and accuracy in various domains. We will discuss examples where AI assists professionals in decision-making processes, automates tedious tasks, and augments human capabilities. By showcasing the positive aspects of AI-human collaboration, we can dispel fears of job displacement and highlight the potential for AI to enhance human potential.

4.2 Drawbacks of AI for Humans

Here, we address the potential drawbacks and challenges that AI poses to human workers. We will discuss the concerns surrounding job displacement and the need for retraining and upskilling. We will explore the psychological and emotional impacts of AI on individuals, such as job insecurity and increased stress levels. Additionally, we will examine the potential for AI to perpetuate social inequality, as certain individuals or groups may face greater challenges in adapting to the AI-driven job market.

4.3 Ethical Considerations in AI Adoption

This subsection focuses on the ethical considerations surrounding AI and its impact on humans. We will discuss the responsible use of AI in areas such as privacy protection, data ethics, and algorithmic transparency. We will examine the potential biases and discrimination that can arise from AI systems and the need for fairness and accountability. By addressing these ethical considerations, we can foster a human-centric approach to AI adoption and ensure that its benefits are shared equitably.

CHAPTER 5: THE FUTURE OF AI AND JOBS

5.1 Predictions for the Future of AI and Jobs

In this section, we will explore predictions for the future of AI and its impact on the job market. We will examine forecasts and expert opinions regarding the growth of AI technologies, the rate of job automation, and the emergence of new job roles. By considering different scenarios and potential trajectories, we can better prepare individuals, organizations, and policymakers for the changing landscape of work.

5.2 The Potential for New Job Creation

Here, we will discuss the potential for AI to create new job opportunities. We will explore emerging fields and industries where AI is driving innovation and the demand for specialized skills. We will examine the role of AI in fostering entrepreneurship, enabling the gig economy, and promoting the growth of small and medium-sized enterprises. By highlighting the potential for job creation, we can inspire individuals to embrace lifelong learning and adaptability in order to thrive in the AI-powered future.

5.3 AI's Transformation of Industries and the Economy

This subsection focuses on how AI has the potential to transform entire industries and reshape the economy. We will explore the disruptive impact of AI on traditional business models, supply chains, and customer experiences. We will discuss the automation of routine tasks, the augmentation of human capabilities, and the potential for AI-driven innovations. By understanding these transformations, we can anticipate the implications for various sectors and proactively shape policies and strategies for a sustainable and inclusive AI-driven economy.

CHAPTER 6: AI AND ETHICAL DECISION-MAKING

6.1 The Ethical Implications of AI in Decision-Making

In this chapter, we delve into the ethical implications of AI in decision-making processes. We examine how AI systems are increasingly being used to make critical decisions in various domains, including healthcare, finance, criminal justice, and more. We discuss the potential benefits of AI in improving e ciency, objectivity, and accuracy in decision-making. However, we also explore the ethical challenges that arise when relying on AI to make consequential choices that impact individuals and society.

6.2 Transparency, Explainability, and Accountability in AI Decision-Making

Here, we address the importance of transparency, explainability, and accountability in AI decision-making. We discuss the need for AI systems to provide clear explanations for their decisions, especially in cases where human lives or fundamental rights are at stake. We explore the challenges of "black box" AI algorithms and the potential for bias and discrimination. By promoting transparency and accountability, we can ensure that AI decisions align with ethical principles, are free from bias, and can be subject to scrutiny and review.

6.3 Balancing Automation and Human Oversight

This section focuses on the delicate balance between automation and human oversight in AI decision- making. We discuss the advantages of AI systems in processing vast amounts of data and identifying patterns that humans may overlook. However, we also emphasize the importance of human judgment,
2values, and ethical considerations in decision-making processes. By incorporating human oversight and
intervention, we can mitigate the risks of undue reliance on AI and ensure that decisions align with societal norms and values.

6.4 The Role of Ethics Frameworks and Guidelines

Here, we explore the development and implementation of ethics frameworks and guidelines for AI decision-making. We discuss the importance of interdisciplinary collaboration involving ethicists, technologists, policymakers, and domain experts in shaping these frameworks. We examine existing initiatives such as the development of ethical AI principles and the integration of ethical considerations into AI development processes. By establishing robust ethics frameworks, we can guide the design and deployment of AI systems that prioritize ethical decision-making and align with societal values.

6.5 Educating and Empowering AI Decision-Makers

In this section, we highlight the importance of educating and empowering AI decision-makers. We discuss the need for AI practitioners, policymakers, and stakeholders to have a deep understanding of the ethical implications of AI in decision-making. We explore the integration of ethics education and training programs to equip individuals with the necessary knowledge and tools to navigate complex ethical challenges. By fostering ethical awareness and competence, we can foster a responsible AI ecosystem where decision- makers prioritize ethical considerations in their use of AI technologies.

CHAPTER 7: EXPLORING AI IN HEALTHCARE

7.1 The Role of AI in Healthcare

This chapter delves into the transformative potential of AI in the healthcare industry. We will explore how AI is revolutionizing medical diagnosis, treatment planning, and patient care. We will discuss the applications of AI in medical imaging, disease prediction, drug discovery, and personalized medicine. By showcasing the advancements in AI-driven healthcare, we can highlight the improved accuracy, efficiency, and accessibility of healthcare services.

7.2 Ethical Considerations in AI Healthcare

Here, we address the ethical considerations associated with the adoption of AI in healthcare. We will discuss issues such as privacy, data security, and the responsible use of patient data. We will explore the challenges of ensuring fairness, transparency, and accountability in AI algorithms used for diagnosis and treatment. By examining these ethical dilemmas, we can foster trust in AI healthcare systems and ensure that patient welfare remains a top priority.

CHAPTER 8: AI AND EDUCATION

8.1 Transforming Education with AI

In this chapter, we explore the potential of AI to revolutionize the field of education. We will discuss AI- powered adaptive learning platforms, intelligent tutoring systems, and personalized learning experiences. We will explore the role of AI in facilitating access to quality education, addressing individual learning needs, and enhancing educational outcomes. By showcasing the benefits of AI in education, we can inspire educators and policymakers to leverage AI technologies for educational advancement.

8.2 Ethical Considerations in AI Education

Here, we address the ethical considerations that arise with the integration of AI in education. We will discuss concerns related to data privacy, algorithmic bias, and the potential for AI to perpetuate educational inequities. We will explore the importance of ensuring transparency, inclusivity, and ethical AI practices in educational settings. By critically examining these considerations, we can create a responsible framework for AI adoption in education.

CHAPTER 9: AI AND FINANCIAL SERVICES

9.1 AI Revolutionizing Financial Services

This chapter focuses on the disruptive potential of AI in the financial services sector. We will explore how AI is transforming areas such as fraud detection, risk assessment, algorithmic trading, and customer service. We will discuss the benefits of AI in improving efficiency, accuracy, and personalized financial solutions. By highlighting the advancements in AI-driven financial services, we can help readers understand the changing landscape of the industry.

9.2 Ethical Considerations in AI Financial Services

Here, we address the ethical considerations associated with the use of AI in financial services. We will discuss the challenges of algorithmic bias, the need for responsible AI governance, and the potential for AI to impact consumer privacy and financial security. We will explore the importance of transparency, fairness

CHAPTER 10: AI AND TRANSPORTATION

10.1 The Impact of AI on Transportation

This chapter explores the transformative impact of AI on the transportation industry. We will discuss the role of AI in autonomous vehicles, traffic management systems, logistics optimization, and predictive maintenance. We will examine how AI can improve safety, efficiency, and sustainability in transportation. By showcasing real-world examples and case studies, we can illustrate the potential of AI to revolutionize the way we travel and transport goods.

10.2 Ethical Considerations in AI Transportation

Here, we address the ethical considerations that arise with the integration of AI in transportation. We will discuss the challenges related to safety, liability, and privacy in the era of autonomous vehicles. We will explore the need for robust regulations, ethical frameworks, and public trust in AI transportation systems. By examining these ethical dilemmas, we can ensure that AI technologies in transportation prioritize human well-being and societal benefits.

CHAPTER 11: AI AND CUSTOMER SERVICE

11.1 Enhancing Customer Service with AI

In this chapter, we explore how AI is revolutionizing customer service across various industries. We will discuss the role of AI-powered chatbots, virtual assistants, and sentiment analysis in delivering personalized and efficient customer experiences. We will examine how AI can streamline customer interactions, automate repetitive tasks, and provide real-time support. By showcasing the benefits of AI in customer service, we can inspire businesses to leverage AI technologies to enhance customer satisfaction.

11.2 Ethical Considerations in AI Customer Service

Here, we address the ethical considerations associated with the use of AI in customer service. We will discuss issues such as privacy, data security, and the responsible use of customer data. We will explore the challenges of ensuring transparency, fairness, and accountability in AI-driven customer service interactions. By examining these ethical concerns, we can promote responsible AI practices that prioritize customer privacy and trust.

CHAPTER 12: AI AND CREATIVE INDUSTRIES

12.1 AI's Influence on Creative Industries

This chapter focuses on the impact of AI on creative fields such as art, music, design, and content creation. We will explore how AI is being used to generate art, compose music, design products, and create digital content. We will discuss the benefits of AI in augmenting human creativity, facilitating new forms of expression, and pushing the boundaries of innovation. By showcasing AI's influence on creative industries, we can inspire artists and creators to embrace AI as a tool for exploration and innovation.

12.2 Ethical Considerations in AI Creative Industries

Here, we address the ethical considerations associated with the use of AI in creative industries. We will discuss issues such as intellectual property rights, authenticity, and the role of human creativity in the face of AI-generated content. We will explore the importance of attribution, fair use, and maintaining a balance between human agency and AI assistance in creative endeavors. By examining these ethical considerations, we can ensure that AI's impact on creative industries aligns with ethical principles and respects the rights and contributions of artists.

CHAPTER 13: AI AND SOCIAL IMPACT

13.1 AI's Role in Addressing Social Challenges

In this chapter, we explore how AI can be leveraged to address pressing social challenges. We will discuss the applications of AI in areas such as healthcare accessibility, poverty alleviation, disaster response, and climate change mitigation. We will examine how AI can enable data-driven decision-making, optimize resource allocation, and empower communities. By showcasing AI's potential for positive social impact, we can inspire individuals, organizations, and policymakers to harness AI technologies for the betterment of society.

13.2 Ethical Considerations in AI Social Impact

Here, we address the ethical considerations associated with the use of AI for social impact. We will discuss issues such as equity, bias, and the need for inclusive AI development We will explore the challenges of ensuring fairness, transparency, and accountability in AI-driven social initiatives. We will discuss the potential risks of exacerbating existing inequalities, reinforcing biases, and infringing on individual rights. By critically examining these ethical considerations, we can develop responsible guidelines and frameworks for deploying AI technologies in social impact projects. It is crucial to prioritize ethical principles, social justice, and the well-being of marginalized communities to harness AI's potential for positive change.

CHAPTER 14: AI AND CYBERSECURITY

14.1 Strengthening Cybersecurity with AI

This chapter focuses on the intersection of AI and cybersecurity. We will explore how AI is used to detect and prevent cyber threats, enhance anomaly detection, and fortify network security. We will discuss the benefits of AI in real-time threat analysis, pattern recognition, and automated response systems. By showcasing the advancements in AI-driven cybersecurity, we can highlight the role of AI in safeguarding digital assets and protecting individuals and organizations from cyberattacks.

14.2 Ethical Considerations in AI Cybersecurity

Here, we address the ethical considerations associated with the use of AI in cybersecurity. We will discuss issues such as privacy, data protection, and the responsible use of AI in surveillance and threat mitigation. We will explore the challenges of maintaining a balance between security needs and individual privacy rights. By examining these ethical dilemmas, we can establish ethical guidelines and practices that prioritize both cybersecurity and the protection of individual rights and freedoms.

CHAPTER 15: AI AND GOVERNANCE

15.1 The Role of AI in Governance

In this chapter, we explore how AI is transforming governance and public administration. We will discuss the applications of AI in areas such as policy-making, decision support systems, and citizen engagement. We will examine the benefits of AI in improving the efficiency, transparency, and effectiveness of governance processes. By showcasing real-world examples of AI in governance, we can illustrate its potential to enhance public services and promote inclusive decision-making.

15.2 Ethical Considerations in AI Governance

Here, we address the ethical considerations associated with the use of AI in governance. We will discuss issues such as accountability, transparency, and the potential for bias in AI-driven decision-making. We will explore the importance of ensuring citizen participation, fairness, and the responsible use of AI in public administration. By examining these ethical concerns, we can establish ethical frameworks that foster trust, inclusivity, and public welfare in AI-driven governance systems.

CHAPTER 16: AI AND THE FUTURE WORKFORCE

16.1 Adapting to the AI-Driven Workforce

This chapter focuses on the evolving landscape of work in the age of AI. We will discuss the impact of AI on jobs, skill requirements, and workforce dynamics. We will explore how individuals and organizations can adapt to the changing nature of work and embrace the opportunities presented by AI technologies. By examining the potential for human-AI collaboration, lifelong learning, and upskilling, we can prepare the future workforce for the AI-driven economy.

16.2 Ethical Considerations in the AI-Driven Workforce

Here, we address the ethical considerations associated with AI's impact on the workforce. We will discuss issues such as job displacement, inequality, and the need for equitable access to AI technologies and opportunities. We will explore the importance of responsible AI adoption, retraining programs, and ensuring a just transition for affected workers. By examining these ethical considerations, we can promote a future workforce that benefits from AI while upholding ethical values and social responsibility.

CHAPTER 17: AI AND PERSONAL PRIVACY

17.1 Balancing Personalization and Privacy

In this chapter, we explore the delicate balance between personalization and privacy in the age of AI. We will discuss the benefits of AI in delivering personalized experiences, customized recommendations, and tailored services. However, we will also delve into the potential risks and challenges to personal privacy that arise with the collection and analysis of vast amounts of personal data. By examining the ethical considerations surrounding data privacy, consent, and data ownership, we can foster a responsible approach to AI that respects individuals' privacy rights.

17.2 Ethical Considerations in AI Personal Privacy

Here, we address the ethical considerations associated with the use of AI and personal privacy. We will discuss the importance of informed consent, transparency in data collection and usage, and the secure storage of personal information. We will explore the risks of data breaches, algorithmic bias, and the potential for manipulation and discrimination based on personal data. By examining these ethical concerns, we can develop robust privacy frameworks and regulations that protect individuals' privacy while reaping the benefits of AI-driven personalization.

CHAPTER 18: AI AND GLOBAL COLLABORATION

18.1 Harnessing AI for Global Collaboration

In this chapter, we explore how AI can facilitate global collaboration and address complex global challenges. We will discuss the applications of AI in areas such as cross-cultural communication, language translation, and data sharing. We will examine how AI can enable diverse teams to collaborate effectively, break down language barriers, and foster cultural understanding. By showcasing examples of AI-powered collaboration platforms and initiatives, we can highlight the potential of AI to bridge global divides and promote cooperation.

18.2 Ethical Considerations in AI Global Collaboration

Here, we address the ethical considerations associated with AI-driven global collaboration. We will discuss issues such as data sovereignty, cultural sensitivity, and the equitable distribution of AI resources and benefits. We will explore the challenges of algorithmic bias in cross-cultural contexts and the potential for AI to reinforce power imbalances. By examining these ethical concerns, we can promote inclusive and responsible AI-driven global collaboration that respects cultural diversity, human rights, and equitable participation.

CHAPTER 19: AI AND THE ENVIRONMENT

19.1 Advancing Environmental Sustainability with AI

This chapter focuses on the role of AI in addressing environmental challenges and promoting sustainability. We will discuss how AI is being used in areas such as climate modeling, renewable energy optimization, resource management, and conservation efforts. We will explore how AI can analyze large datasets, identify patterns, and support evidence-based decision-making for environmental protection. By showcasing the potential of AI to accelerate progress towards environmental sustainability, we can inspire individuals, organizations, and policymakers to leverage AI technologies for a greener future.

19.2 Ethical Considerations in AI Environmental Applications

Here, we address the ethical considerations associated with the use of AI in environmental applications. We will discuss issues such as data transparency, accountability, and the potential for AI to exacerbate environmental injustices. We will explore the importance of responsible data collection, algorithmic transparency, and equitable access to environmental benefits. By examining these ethical concerns, we can ensure that AI-driven environmental initiatives uphold ethical principles, protect vulnerable communities, and promote long-term environmental well-being.

CHAPTER 20: AI AND THE FUTURE OF HUMANITY

20.1 Navigating the Impact of AI on Society

In this final chapter, we explore the broader implications of AI on the future of humanity. We will discuss the societal, economic, and ethical challenges that arise as AI continues to advance. We will examine the potential benefits and risks of AI, including issues related to employment, inequality, and human autonomy. By considering the far-reaching implications of AI, we can engage in thoughtful discussions and shape policies and practices that prioritize the well-being and flourishing of humanity

20.2 Ethical Considerations in Shaping the Future of AI

Here, we address the critical ethical considerations in shaping the future of AI. We will discuss the importance of responsible AI development, governance, and regulation. We will explore the need for transparency, explainability, and accountability in AI systems. Additionally, we will examine the ethical dilemmas surrounding the development of artificial general intelligence (AGI) and its potential impact on human society. By considering these ethical considerations, we can work towards a future where AI technologies are developed and deployed in a manner that aligns with human values, respects fundamental rights, and promotes the common good.

20.3 Fostering Collaboration and Multidisciplinary Approaches

To navigate the complexities of AI's impact on society, collaboration across diverse disciplines is crucial. In this section, we emphasize the importance of multidisciplinary approaches in AI development and deployment. We explore how collaborations between AI researchers, ethicists, policymakers, social scientists, and other stakeholders can lead to more holistic and responsible AI solutions. By fostering a collaborative environment, we can combine technological expertise with ethical, social, and legal perspectives to address the complex challenges and maximize the benefits of AI technologies.

20.4 Empowering Responsible AI Citizenship

As AI technologies become increasingly pervasive, it is essential to cultivate responsible AI citizenship. This section highlights the role of individuals, organizations, and policymakers in shaping the future of AI. We discuss the importance of ethical AI education, promoting digital literacy, and fostering public engagement in AI-related discussions. By empowering individuals with the knowledge and tools to understand and critically assess AI technologies, we can ensure that AI is developed, deployed, and governed in ways that prioritize human values, social impact, and long-term sustainability.

20.5 Looking Ahead: The Promise and Responsibility of AI

In the final section, we reflect on the promise and responsibility of AI. We acknowledge the tremendous potential of AI technologies to solve complex problems, improve lives, and advance human civilization. However, we also recognize the responsibility we bear in navigating the ethical, social, and economic implications of AI. We emphasize the need for ongoing dialogue, research, and policy development to shape AI technologies in a manner that reflects our collective values and aspirations. By embracing the promise of AI with a deep sense of responsibility, we can steer its development and deployment towards a future that benefits all of humanity.

Conclusion

In this comprehensive exploration of AI and its ethical considerations, we have examined the transformative potential of AI across various domains. From healthcare and education to finance, transportation, and creative industries, AI is reshaping our world. However, as we embrace AI's capabilities, we must also address the ethical challenges that arise. Privacy, bias, accountability, transparency, and inclusivity are among the key considerations that must guide the responsible development and deployment of AI technologies.

By delving into these ethical considerations in each chapter, we have aimed to foster a nuanced understanding of the complex interplay between AI and society. We have highlighted the need for robust ethical frameworks, regulatory measures, and interdisciplinary collaboration to navigate the ethical landscape of AI effectively.

As AI continues to evolve and shape our future, it is incumbent upon us as individuals, organizations, and societies to make conscious and responsible choices. By engaging in critical dialogue, upholding ethical values, and prioritizing the well-being of individuals and communities, we can harness the transformative power of AI while mitigating its potential risks.

In conclusion, the ethical considerations surrounding AI demand our attention, and it is through our collective efforts that we can shape an AI-powered future that aligns with our shared values and promotes the betterment of humanity.

EPILOGUE

As we conclude this journey through the realm of AI and its profound impact on jobs and society, it is clear that we stand at the precipice of a new era. The AI revolution has brought about unprecedented changes, challenging traditional notions of work, human capabilities, and the very fabric of our existence. Throughout this book, we have explored the multifaceted aspects of AI, delving into its potential, limitations, and the ethical considerations that surround its deployment.

The future holds both promise and uncertainty. AI has already demonstrated its potential to enhance productivity, automate repetitive tasks, and revolutionize industries. We have witnessed its applications in healthcare, education, finance, manufacturing, transportation, entertainment, retail, agriculture, energy, government, marketing, and beyond. It has become an integral part of our daily lives, shaping the way we live, work, and interact with the world.

However, the rise of AI has also raised concerns about job displacement, algorithmic bias, privacy, security, and the ethical dilemmas associated with autonomous decision-making systems. As we move forward, it is crucial to address these challenges and ensure that AI is developed and utilized in a responsible and inclusive manner.

The impact of AI on the job market will continue to evolve, requiring individuals and organizations to adapt and acquire new skills. The future workforce will need to embrace lifelong learning and cultivate a flexible mindset to thrive in a world where human-machine collaboration becomes the norm.

While the road ahead may be paved with uncertainty, one thing remains certain: the power of human ingenuity and creativity. AI, at its core, is a tool that amplifies our abilities, augments our decision-making processes, and opens up new frontiers of discovery. It is a catalyst for innovation and progress.

As we bid farewell to this exploration of AI and its far-reaching consequences, let us remember that the true power lies not in the technology itself, but in our ability to harness it for the betterment of humanity. Let us continue to question, to push boundaries, and to strive for a future where AI serves as a force for good, creating a world that is equitable, inclusive, and sustainable.

May this book serve as a guide and an inspiration to all those who embark on the path of understanding and shaping the AI revolution. Together, let us navigate the complexities, seize the opportunities, and build a future where humans and machines coexist harmoniously, ushering in an era of unprecedented progress and shared prosperity.

With deep gratitude,

[imrtst]

AFTERWORD

Congratulations! You have reached the end of this enlightening journey into the world of AI and its profound implications for jobs and society. We hope that this book has provided you with valuable insights, sparked your curiosity, and encouraged you to ponder the future that awaits us in the age of intelligent machines.

As we conclude our exploration, it is important to remember that the field of AI is constantly evolving. New advancements, breakthroughs, and debates will shape the landscape in the years to come. We encourage you to stay curious, stay informed, and continue to engage in discussions surrounding AI's impact on our lives.

The future is not predetermined. It is up to us, as individuals and as a collective, to shape the trajectory of AI and harness its potential for the benefit of all. Let us remain vigilant, proactive, and guided by a strong moral compass as we navigate the complexities that lie ahead.

We extend our sincere gratitude to you, the reader, for embarking on this intellectual voyage with us. It is through your curiosity and open-mindedness that we can collectively drive positive change and create a future that embraces the best of what AI has to offer while safeguarding the values that make us human.

Remember, the power to shape the future is in our hands. Let us embrace the opportunities, address the challenges, and continue to explore the vast potential of AI in a way that aligns with our shared vision of a prosperous and inclusive society.

Thank you for joining us on this transformative journey.

Sincerely,

[imrtst]

ABOUT THE AUTHOR

Imrtst

-designer, writer and expert in artificial intelligence.
-Designer with a focus on creativity and uniqueness.
-Seamlessly combines technical expertise with storytelling.
-Deep understanding of the impact of AI on industries and society.
-Advocate for ethical and responsible AI development.
-Engaging and informative content creator on AI-related topics.
-Constantly stays updated with the latest advancements in the field.
-Provides a fresh perspective and innovative ideas.
-Committed to comprehensive understanding and inspiring -readers.
-Multidisciplinary background in writing and design.

BOOKS BY THIS AUTHOR

Mars Unveiled: Elon Musk's Quest For A New Frontier

Discover the extraordinary vision of Elon Musk and his plans for Mars colonization in "Elon Musk's Mars Plans: Challenges, Technologies, and the Struggle for Life on the Red Planet." This captivating book explores the obstacles, technological advancements, and profound implications of venturing beyond Earth. Delve into the challenges of establishing a sustainable human colony on Mars, the potential benefits of colonization, and the remarkable technologies being developed by SpaceX. Uncover the struggles and conflicts that may arise, and envision the future of Mars colonization and its impact on space exploration and humanity. Join this epic adventure and explore the boundless possibilities of Mars.

Awakening The Inner Self: Exploring The Path To Enlightenment

"Awakening the Inner Self: Exploring the Path to Enlightenment" is a profound and illuminating book that invites readers on a transformative journey of self-discovery and spiritual awakening. With deep insight and wisdom, the author explores the inner realms of consciousness, guiding readers on a path towards enlightenment. Through ancient teachings, practical exercises, and profound contemplations, this book offers a roadmap to unlock the hidden potential within and connect with the true essence of one's being. From understanding the nature of the mind to exploring the depths of meditation and self-inquiry, each chapter provides a stepping stone towards greater self-awareness and inner peace. "Awakening the Inner Self" is a powerful guide that empowers readers to embark on a transformative journey and discover the limitless possibilities that lie within.

www.ingramcontent.com/pod-product-compliance
Lightning Source LLC
Chambersburg PA
CBHW070134230526
45472CB00004B/1527